Broken BREAD

3rd Collection

Reinhard Bonnke

Broken Bread · 3rd Collection
English

Copyright © Full Flame GmbH 2005
ISBN 3-937180-19-2

1. Edition, 1. Print
11,000 copies

Cover Design: Isabelle Brasche
Backcover photo: Rob Birkbeck
Frontcover photo & Typeset: Roland Senkel

Publisher:

Full Flame GmbH
Postfach 60 05 95
60335 Frankfurt am Main
Germany

info@fullflame.com
www.fullflame.com

Printed in Germany

Table of Contents

Twice as much

Because of the blood of my covenant with you,
return to your fortress, o prisoners of hope,
even now I announce that I will restore
twice as much to you.

Zechariah 9:11-12

Twice as much! Double! Multiply! Increase! Abound! That is Scripture talk. The Bible begins that way, three times in the first chapter God's order is to 'multiply', giving us a picture of productive life, clothing the world with beauty, God's garment of glory. We read how things 'increase with the increase of God', an ever widening and deepening river, nothing threadbare, worn out, patched up, but *"the goodness of the Lord fills the whole earth"* God doesn't want the world to think of him as poverty stricken, just scraping along, an impression church meanness has sometimes produced.

The Bible is the most positive book in the world. It has no room for terms like subtract, halve, cut back, and reduce. In the heavenly music they are off-notes. But 'increase' and 'increased' occur over 160 times. The Creator's method of organic growth is by the process of the doubling of cells over and over in the DNA helix. He is the ceaseless Giver, an endlessly flowing stream. He pours himself out like the sun giving light.

Zechariah's words above come from the year 536 BC when King Cyrus sent Judean captives back to their homeland and Jerusalem. The prophets Zechariah and Haggai encouraged them with the words of the Lord. They faced impoverished desolation and had to start from scratch to make a living and build necessary homes. But they gave priority to fitting up their dwellings in luxurious style, while the house of God was not even built. The Temple was vital to national unity, and no mere token. It was needed as the heart of their relationship with God. But it was neglected and that brought inevitable repercussions. The prophet said they sowed much but reaped little and put their money into a bag with holes. Food shortages harassed them, prosperity eluded them. That was never how God wanted it. He delights in 'double'.

> Where anybody wishes to give, God sees they have something to give. He makes us channels of provision. He calls us to exercise the grace of giving.

The prophet said *"Consider your ways!"* Recognize God! Put first things first and attend to the central pivot of their national existence! When they did Haggai pointed out that from that day somehow things got better. Zechariah predicted God would revive their fortunes *"I will restore twice as much to you."* It is a matter of universal experience that there is a law of sowing and reaping, and sowing spiritual goodness brings material goodness.

I observed that Paul the apostle was not squeamish about offerings to God. Using the same two or three words time after time, like hammer blows, he emphasized, *"just as you excel* [abound] *in all things, in faith, in speech, in know-ledge. See that you also excel* [or abound] *in this grace of giving. God loves a cheerful giver. And God is able to make all grace excel* [or abound] *to you so that in all things at all times, having all that you need, you will excel* [abound] *in all good works."* (2 Corinthians 8:7, 9:8) Paul, being aware of their pride in spiritual gifts, prophecy, tongues, healings, he told them to 'excel' and then said exercise also this cha-risma of giving also.

Where anybody wishes to give, God sees they have something to give, not only money but effort, time and prayer. He makes us channels of provision. He calls us to exercise the grace of giving. Called to give! Giving is God's joy and our earthly circumstances are an opportunity to share in his joy.

> Giving is God's joy and our earthly circumstances are an opportunity to share in his joy.

In the law of Deuteronomy 21:17, a first-born son should have twice as much from his father as other sons. The Lord called Israel his first-born son. It was a coded promise to Israel that they would prosper, receive double beyond other nations. God promised to bless Abraham, and in his case he gained wealth and possessions. Well, did ever God bless people by making them poor? It reminds me of Joseph in Egypt setting twice as much food at the table for Benjamin his blood brother as for the other ten. That is the style of the royal house of heaven also, a heaped up plate, a loaded table, an overflowing cup. *"You prepare a table before me"*.

> Our heavenly Father favours sinners, us, the fallen sons of fallen Adam. What Elisha asked is given us, a double portion of his Spirit. The bounty of God is so all-embracing.

Mosaic laws may sometimes legislate for exceptions. Here's one instance anyhow, and with good reason. It lays down the hypothetical case of a man with two wives, one hated, the other loved. If his hated wife bears him a son first, the boy is entitled to a double portion. It should not be given to the first-born of the favourite wife. The principle is quite astonishing, Certainly Jacob did not follow it with Joseph and Benjamin. The first-born should be accepted for full sonship favour and not lose out because of prejudice or parentage. This sounds like Jesus saying *"If ye then being evil give good gifts to your children how much more will your heavenly Father give the Holy Spirit to them that ask!"* Our heavenly Father favours sinners, us, the fallen sons of fallen Adam. What Elisha asked is given us, a double portion of his Spirit. The bounty of God is so all-embracing.

Being "graced"

God has nothing to do with disfavour. The Mosaic rule is reflected in Ephesians 1:6 *"To the praise of the glory of his grace, wherein he has made us accepted in the beloved"*. The first born son of the hated wife had to be 'accepted in the beloved'. Paul uses a special word here found only twice in the New Testament. Literally it would read God had 'graced us in the beloved.' The same word was used by the angel at the Annunciation, Luke 1:28. Gabriel appeared to Mary the virgin and said she was 'graced'. The usual English translation is "highly favoured". God 'highly favoured' Mary, and "highly favours" us, accepting us into the 'beloved' or 'the one beloved'. No discrimination.

The NIV translation is "the one he loves", we are accepted in his beloved. The Lord spoke from heaven saying Christ was his "beloved son" (Matthew 3:17). We are favoured in him, or along with him, or we inherit with the beloved one as heirs of God (Galatians 4:7).

Equally, Israel was his loved son. Malachi 1:2-3 *"Was not Jacob Esau's brother?" the Lord says, "Yet I have loved Jacob, but Esau have I hated"*. We gentiles who do not descend from Jacob, were the 'hated', remaining in darkness while God made his love known to Jacob, crooked though he was. But in Christ the 'hated' children, like the son of the hated wife in Deuteronomy, are accepted in the beloved, and we become fellow heirs with Israel of all God's favours. It was to Corinth, a Roman city, that Paul declared they were the 'highly favoured'.

It is high favour because highly undeserved like Jacob was. Yet a girl in the tribe of Jacob

There's no such thing as a deserved favour. It would be a right, not a favour. They talk much about human rights, but we have no human right to acceptance into the beloved, whether Jacob or the son of the father. It is all of grace, a gift, or rather multi-gifts.

cradled Christ in her arms. There's no such thing as a deserved favour. It would be a right, not a favour. They talk much about human rights, but we have no human right to acceptance into the beloved, whether Jacob or the son of the father. It is all of grace, a gift, or rather multi-gifts.

Unlimited in God

The prophet Elijah had a servant, Elisha who asked Elijah *"Let me inherit a double portion of your spirit!"* Now, Elijah made his appearances in Israel with a series of dramatic miracles, mainly judgments. Elisha knew Elijah would soon be removed from the scene, and did not want Elijah's ministry to be cut off. So to continue the glory of God in Israel he asked Elijah for a 'double portion', as Elijah's spiritual son. Elijah said it was 'hard', actually impossible for Elijah, but God did it.

> Jesus said that as the bringers of the gospel their spirit would be rich in the endowments of God's grace and goodness.

Perhaps Elisha hoped just for the elder son's share, but God does not need to share anything, as if he had limited means. He poured out upon Elisha more than he asked or thought, giving him a ministry double Elijah's miracle ministry, and also different marked by God's goodness and grace. Elijah was always Israel's favourite prophet because of their desire for judgment upon their enemies, as so often expressed in the book of Psalms. Elijah had personalized that attitude, but Elisha manifested mercy.

The angel told Zacharias the father of John the Baptist that John would come in the spirit and power of Elijah. His preaching reflected the Elijah disposition of judgment. Christ's disciples showed a similar spirit wanting to call fire from heaven (like Elijah upon a hostile Samaritan village). Jesus said *"You don't know what manner of spirit you are"*, meaning that as the bringers of the gospel their spirit would be rich in the endowments of God's grace and goodness. John the Baptist wondered if he had got it right as Christ brought no destruction annihilating Israel's foes, but wrought acts of immense grace and goodness, in the spirit of Elisha. Christ nevertheless sent John great encouragement, assuring him that he was the one John expected, though God was not all judgment.

> That's God's way:
> Never calculating
> but extravagant,
> doubling double
> over and over.

We learn – slowly. Elisha learned to believe God for double. Jesus showed John the Baptist more than he prophesied or Elisha dreamed. That's God's way. Never calculating but extravagant, doubling double over and over. Moses had the Spirit, and then the 70 elders. When one or two others received it Joshua was anxious, as if there was only so much to be had. But Joel spoke of the Spirit upon 'all flesh'. Its first realization came for 120 on the day of Pentecost, next the 3,000, then the 5,000, then spreading away to Samaria, Corinth, Ephesus. Ezekiel foresaw the unlimited in God, pictured as water, waters to the ankles, to the thighs, then waters to swim in. Ever increasing blessing, rains, monsoons, floods, and waterfalls!

To be like God we have to give. Without irreverence I think of God as an extremist, an extremist in love overcoming extreme evil, giving everything he had at the cross. What extravagance! We are worth nothing except what he paid to redeem us.

> God is an extremist, an extremist in love overcoming extreme evil, giving everything he had at the cross.
> What extravagance! We are worth nothing except what he paid to redeem us.

He wrapped the robe of his everlasting love around the shoulders of this prodigal planet – what a costly and rich robe that was, but that is God, liberal beyond the narrow concepts of our little minds. How can people sing "Fill my cup Lord!" What sort of Bible theology or view of God is that? Cup? Why – Christ's very first miracle was a divine gesture of lavish extravagance – 120 gallons of the finest wine. His promise is streams of living waters. "Indulge yourself in the Lord!" Revel in the munificence of God. Double? Yes, and God doubles all the time.

Signs and Wonders

Signs and wonders. That is a phrase straight out of the Bible. In fact, you won't find it in the sacred writings of other religions. Why not? Because signs and wonders are not part of other religions. They have their place in Bible-based belief. If the Lord had a shop in the High Street, the sign hanging up outside to tell people what kind of business he was running would read "wonders". It would be the only shop in the street specialising in miracles.

It is absurd to say that miracles are impossible, conceit in fact. No one has enough knowledge to be able to make such a statement. A sceptic is really an arrogant know-all. If we were to measure human ignorance in cubic feet, we would probably run out of numbers. Let's be honest – we simply do not understand existence, what it is, or how it came about. Of course, we have evidence of certain things and hypotheses about others, but even then we have nowhere near exhausted all the things that exist for us to learn about.

Charles Dickens was a writer of immense imagination, but he could not have predicted the advent of television, computers or men on the moon – all things that came about within a century of his death. Einstein even declared that nuclear fission could never be a source of power. Now we know otherwise. My car is navigated by satellite through city streets, which I find absolutely amazing even as I sit behind the wheel. Could it be that those who think that

> The Bible presents a God who is busy moving across chaos, bringing life and order, spinning the sun, moon and stars into orbit, creating seas and continents.

there is nothing left to learn are committing the same kind of error as Einstein and others, famous and not?

Addressing Agrippa's royal court, Paul asked, *"Why should any of you consider it incredible that God raises the dead?"* (Acts 26:8). Why indeed? That question is unanswerable.

Of course, God is bound to be a mystery or he would not be God. God is by definition supernatural. Just open the Bible anywhere and the supernatural is there behind the events as they unfold.

Creation – the greatest of all Signs and Wonders

The miraculous is God's stock in trade – and I do not mean miracles of healing only. Of course God can heal all sorts of diseases, including headaches, but, for me, his powers do not start or end there. God is not an alternative to aspirin; he is the God who made heaven and earth. That very fact is the subject of the entire first two chapters to the Bible.

God is, in fact, greater than the signs of his existence. Signs are given to serve his purposes, not ours. And he has more in mind than to astonish us or to provide us with a few moments of excitement. Signs simply point towards him, like a road sign telling us which way to take. They are hints of God's greatness, his footprints on the grass showing us where he has been.

The Bible does not present God as the sum of the impressions, which came to some meditating mystic. Neither is he a shadowy deity in a mythical heaven, and even less a logical theory. The Bible presents a God who is busy moving across chaos, bringing life and order, spinning the sun, moon and stars into orbit, creating seas and continents.

To believe in God the Creator leaves us no alternative but to believe in a God of miracles. The God who put the Himalayas where he wanted can hardly be baffled by somebody's bad knee. He wields endless power, far beyond measure. To a God like that, signs and wonders are no problem.

> Once the work of Creation was complete, God did not sit down and do nothing or take early retirement. He is still around today.

When he created the world, God released infinite life-giving energies. He has kept it all well within his control ever since. Once the work of Creation was complete, he did not sit down and do nothing or take early retirement. Nor did he go into self-imposed exile a long way away from his world. He is still around today. He handled material at the beginning of time, has he only handled spiritual things ever since? Wouldn't that be rather out of character, inconsistent? The work of the Creator cannot be reduced to mere spirituality no matter how hard some might try.

After Creation, a Miracle with an earthly and a spiritual Dimension

Hardly had man and woman been installed in the new world than they upset everything. But God acted immediately. He is not the author of confusion; from the beginning of time he determined not to let the prevailing darkness and chaos remain. Whatever needed putting right was the kind of challenge to which he rose. Nothing has changed! When Adam and his wife took that fatal step which changed the course of human history, God immediately set about creating order out of disorder and rebellion. Any act of God in this world is supernatural.

God's first act after Creation was this example of salvation, which called for both spiritual and physical intervention. If we talk about signs and wonders, we must include salvation. Jesus saves. The idea that he can save a soul and ignore the man or the woman is unacceptable. When God saves, he saves people, not just their hidden facet, their spiritual being. Every born-again person is a sign and wonder, an indication of God's presence and evidence of his power. To me, God's glorious salvation is the greatest wonder of all and the most powerful sign of God's character.

Signs and Wonders typify Bible-based Religion

Christianity has two sides, the spiritual and the physical. That is the basic revelation and what makes Christianity revolutionary. Jesus Christ is the Saviour, Healer, Baptiser in the Spirit and the Coming King. Each of those cardinal truths involves the physical. Signs and wonders are inherent in the full gospel message.

For many people faith has been confined to the realm of the spiritual. Any physical manifestation of God in action has had opponents who have declared signs of God's presence to be "of the flesh" or even of the devil. Critics have said that we should stress the fruit of the Spirit, not the gifts. However, the Bible does not hesitate to speak about gifts. Even the critics claim the Bible as the authority on which they base their beliefs. How, then, can it be wrong to talk about the very things that we find in that great book?

Thanks to the working of the Holy Spirit, the Christian church is coming round to seeing this. There are still those who have a phobia about any physical manifestations, but they are a shrinking minority. Truth cannot be suppressed forever. The Holy Spirit will not be quenched forever by unbelief.

> When God saves,
> he saves people,
> not just their hidden facet,
> their spiritual being.

In Biblical times, people saw God at work. They knew him as a being who did things, not as some professor of metaphysics in an ivory tower. Other religions are based on subjective experiences of imperfect men who claimed to have heard voices, had dreams and visions and went into trances. The Biblical foundation for belief has none of that. The God of the Bible is described in terms of his deeds. His many titles indicate what he did and what he does. In fact, that forms the basis of the Christian creed, our statement of faith. It starts with a sort of brief history of Christ: *"I believe in God Almighty, maker of heaven and earth,"* we say. *"And in Jesus Christ his only son our Lord, who was … born …, suffered under Pontius Pilate, was crucified, dead, and buried … he rose again."*

> *"You are the God who performs miracles."* (Psalm 77:14)

The message of Christ was not irrelevant to the suffering of those who listened to what he had to say. He embodied the message from heaven about God's love for humankind, real palpable, breathing, moving and certainly alive. Today, as then, he is our message, that of a living faith. The messengers are living agents, channels of the same divine power and love which moved Christ.

If we want to get through to God, to ring him up as it were, then the book lists him, as Psalm 77:14 says, as *"the God who performs miracles"*. We have to know exactly who we want to ring, otherwise we will get a wrong number or no answer. The Bible encourages us to dial God's number: *"Call to me and I will answer you and tell you great and unsearchable things you do not know"* (Jeremiah 33:3).

The first disciples saw Christ healing the sick and were amazed. Hope took hold of them and they advanced into the dark world of universal paganism with the brilliance of the gospel light flashing with the miracle signs. The work to be done today is every bit as great and still needs the miraculous. If we preach the Word, that is what we should expect.

Signs and Wonders are earthly Acts performed by God's Spirit

There is an important basic truth about the Holy Spirit that is not always acknowledged. His work is usually physical or links the spiritual and the physical; very rarely is it spiritual only. When miracles occurred, the Old Testament credited them to the Spirit of the Lord. The physical world was the Spirit's special sphere of operation.

In the New Testament it is the same. When Jesus healed the sick we are told that he was

When we accept Jesus Christ as our Lord and Saviour, his Spirit takes up residence within us and makes our physical bodies his temples.

"anointed with the Holy Spirit and power" (Acts 10:38). The wind, fire and tongues of the Day of Pentecost were seen as typical of the Holy Spirit. The physical is still his sphere of activity today; God does not change his policy. If we believe in the Holy Spirit then we should believe in his characteristic work, signs and wonders. The Holy Spirit is God at work in this world. When we accept Jesus Christ as our Lord and Saviour, his Spirit takes up residence within us and makes our physical bodies his temples.

Signs and Wonders are the Hallmark of a living God

Unless God acts, how do we know he is there? A living God will surely show that he is alive. Obviously, if God acts, it is supernatural. Some say that he acts in and through the natural. I am sure he does, and in the Old Testament that is how everybody thought. But even then there were some deeds that stood out as wonders, supernatural interventions. The greatest was his deliverance of Israel from Egypt, when, for instance, the waters of the Red Sea rolled back like a carpet to let the people through. Nowadays, with our understanding of natural processes, we know a direct act of God when we see one. The Creator can still create and work on his own creation. In any case, God's power underpins all things.

Jesus said, *"These signs will accompany those who believe"* (Mark 16:17). Miracles have always been a vital confirmation of the gospel. They reveal what God is. They are proof of his existence and his power. There is no such thing as an evil miracle. People talk about what the devil does, but true wonders are benefits, blessings bestowed on us by God himself. God is a living God, a miracle God, the God who made heaven and earth by stupendous miracles. He does not intend to hide from us completely. Indeed, he reveals his very nature whenever he performs a healing miracle. That is God, the God who made all the wonders of nature, all its rich variety and goodness, enough to satisfy every living

> People talk about what the devil does, but true wonders are benefits, blessings bestowed on us by God himself.

> Signs and wonderes should be a standing feature of all church life, a permanent witness to the world.
> A church without signs and wonders is not the church Jesus planned.

creature. The God who works miracles like that shows that he is the same God as in the beginning of the Bible.

I do not believe that these signs are reserved for pioneer evangelists; they should be a standing feature of all church life, a permanent witness to the world. A church without signs and wonders is not the church Jesus planned.

Signs and Wonders make the Bible what it is

The miraculous is the hallmark of the Bible. The supernatural is the glue, which binds the Scriptures together. The book would be no more than scattered pages and scraps of paper if you tore out everything based on the miraculous.

Having said that, in the Old Testament actual miracles were comparatively rare. Yet every reference to God alludes to his miraculous power. In those days the Holy Spirit came upon individuals when they had to perform special tasks, as happened to Moses, Samuel, Samson and the prophets. But since Jesus came down to earth and later ascended to glory, the Holy Spirit has been outpoured on all people – indeed, on whoever asks. The Spirit of the prophets is now being given to young and old, men and women, just as Joel foretold.

The Holy Spirit has been outpoured on all people – indeed, on whoever asks. The Spirit of the prophets is now being given to young and old, men and women, just as Joel foretold.

The New Testament begins in what we call modern times, recorded historic times, the days of the Roman Empire, and that is when miracles became common. As soon as Jesus arrived on the scene there were wholesale healings. They did not cease when Jesus died on the Cross but continued from the hands of the disciples; the promise was that they would continue to the end of the age. Rationalists have tried to write a life of Christ without miracles, but they are trying to build a wall without bricks. They have not yet succeeded and are never likely to. Meanwhile, most modern scholars admit that Jesus was a wonder worker.

Signs and Wonders should flow from the Body of Christ today

The gospels record how God sent his Son, and Jesus' great works of healing were works, which God sent him to do. Jesus said, *"As the Father has sent me, I am sending you"* (John 20:21). The will of the Father has not changed. His compassion and mercy on the sick and afflicted were signs of what God is like. In those days long ago healing was not a special offer or a kind of sales gimmick. It was a revelation of God's character. If Jesus Christ is the same yesterday, today and forever, as the Bible says, then the Jesus in glory is no different from the Jesus of Galilee.

All that holds true today. Jesus has the same compassion and the same power as he did when he walked the earth. The main difference is that he no longer has hands to touch the sick, a voice to speak healing, or feet to bring him into streets and homes. So he sends men and women.

They are his hands and voice and feet. The body of Jesus is his Church, of which he is the head. The hands and voice and feet obey the head.

Jesus sends men and women. They are his hands and voice and feet. The body of Jesus is his Church, of which he is the head. The hands and voice and feet obey the head.

"You have a mighty arm," says Scripture in Psalm 89:13. The Church is the living extension of that mighty arm. However imperfect we may be in this imperfect world, we are still the agents of omnipotence and of divine love, with the task of demonstrating that God cares. As Jesus' disciples, filled with the same Spirit that anointed Jesus, we are to do the same work. Jesus said, *"Anyone who has faith in me will do what I have been doing. He will do even greater things than these"* (John 14:12). They are "greater" because God is not limited to one pair of hands or to one voice; Christians moving everywhere carry the same blessings and love.

Human beings have no natural healing powers. Signs and wonders are not signs of human power, but of God. Signs and wonders are God's signature, impossible to forge. The magicians of ancient Egypt worked magic when Moses challenged them. They tossed sticks on the ground, which became snakes. Moses cast his rod on the ground and it became a serpent that devoured the magician's snakes.

No other god can compete with the Creator. When the Lord delivered Israel out of Egypt we read that he executed judgement against all the gods of Egypt. Among their gods were the river Nile and the sun. God the Creator turned the waters of that river red like blood and blacked out the sun for days. The practitioners of the occult have challenged us during many of our evangelistic campaigns, but they were unable to penetrate the shield of God around us. Naked witches have danced all night round my hotel to cast a spell on me and stop the preaching of Jesus, but it was futile. When we preach Jesus, the people possessed by evil spirits cry out and are delivered.

When we conducted our campaign in Lagos in November 2000, we asked each night how many had been healed the previous night and thousands upon thousands raised their hands.

Signs and Wonders are Evidence of the true and living God

We read in John chapter 3 that Nicodemus, a member of the Jewish ruling authority, came to Jesus "at night". Those words have a double meaning. The visit took place in the dark but this man was in the dark and it showed in what he said. Jesus had to teach him.

One thing is interesting. Nicodemus said, *"No one could perform the miraculous signs you are doing if God were not with him"* (John 3:2). He was right, but he was also confused. He was right because he was talking to Jesus Christ, the Son of God, and God was indeed with him, although not as God is with others. Jesus performed miracles by his own will because God was with him.

Let us be absolutely clear about one thing: God does not help us to heal the sick. No ordinary man can even start to perform wonders. Our task is to lay on hands or to pray, but God alone heals. When we see the deaf and blind restored during our campaigns, we ask

> God does not help us to heal the sick. No ordinary man can even start to perform wonders. Our task is to lay on hands or to pray, but God alone heals.

them, "Who healed you?" The answer is "Jesus". We can do some things, such as preach the Word, and God helps us, but we cannot heal. Nonetheless, God has sent us to take healing from him to the afflicted world. The signs and wonders are not signs of our holiness, but of God at work.

Human beings convey healing. They do not create it and are not its source. They are like water mains carrying the streams of God's life. We do not contribute one drop to the water of life; we are just the pipes through which it travels, God's living conduits carrying streams of mercy to a thirsty world.

Once Jesus healed a leper who wondered whether the Lord would even bother with someone like him (Matthew 8), saying, *"I am willing. Be clean!"* That is an expression of his sovereign will, a declaration of God's will and purpose. Jesus said he did what the Father does – what Jesus did God did with him. God revealed his sovereign purposes

> Signs and wonders are not signs of our holiness, but of God at work.

in Christ in that *"I am willing"* and his purposes stand fast forever. His will does not waver about. It is not unpredictable. God is faithful and keeps faith with us. He shows us what he is and never deviates. And one of the things he is is the healer. He reveals himself by signs and wonders, the mark of his presence. They are not signs of our special personality, our special technique or our knowledge. The only knowledge we need is not intellectual but knowledge of him, which we gain by living with him.

Signs and Wonders need both God and People

Our responsibility is to be plumbed into the reservoirs of heaven. People are dying of spiritual thirst. They can drink, but we must bring them water. Or, to use a different metaphor and talk of power, we must be wired up to the great dynamo of God and the power stations of Calvary and the Resurrection from which currents flow. It is no use trying to switch on and heal the sick unless we are already connected by faith.

Signs and wonders, the power of God, are constantly available when needed. They are not for those times when we are sitting comfortably by the fireside, but are vital out in the world of need. Praying is vital, but it can all too easily become cosy and comfortable. We may perhaps pray together as an excuse to enjoy one another's company. It is easy to ask God to do something, but God is asking us to do something. As he said to Moses, we have to get up and go forward.

Signs and wonders are for the battlefield, for challenging the devil and all his works. They are not to be indulged in as a kind of hobby, a spare-time interest, an alternative to sport, music or games. They are gifts which God wishes to distribute to the neediest cause on earth, people. We are not the donors, merely the delivery boys.

> The power of God is constantly available when needed. It is not for those times when we are sitting comfortably by the fireside, but is vital out in the world of need.

The list of gifts of the Spirit in 1 Corinthians 12 includes gifts of healing for the sick and it is our job to hand them out. We cannot generate or manufacture healings but God will allow us to give his gifts to the sick just as Peter said to the cripple at the temple gate: *"What I have I give you. In the name of Jesus Christ of Nazareth, walk"* (Acts 3:6).

Signs and Wonders point to God not to Men

Peter and John saw a cripple at the gate to the temple and gave him healing in the name of Jesus. The cripple walked, a crowd gathered, and looked at the two apostles as if they were wonder-workers. But Peter hastened to make things clear. *"Why do you stare at us,"* he asked, *"as if by our own power or godliness we had made this man walk?"* (Acts 3:12). Peter was surely conscious of his failure as a human being. He had denied so much as knowing Jesus when the Lord was arrested only a matter of weeks

> To think that when a healing takes place God is signalling his approval of our holiness is an offence to the One who redeemed us.

previously. But the grace of God overwhelms failure and turned Peter into a man we still talk about today.

We cannot generate power by our own holiness and virtue. So many say precisely that and yet write books and preach sermons telling us what we have to do to gain God's power. They are constantly finding new reasons why they lack power. I certainly welcome books telling us how to seek holiness and to be like Jesus, but it is a different thing to promise power as the reward. Power is not a prize at the end of a marathon. We need power at the start if we are to run the marathon for God. Paul was shocked when he found the Galatians talking the language of power by good deeds. In the most urgent of all his letters, he wrote, *"Does God give you his Spirit and work miracles among you because you observe the law, or because you believe what you heard?"* (Galatians 3:5).

We have no inherent healing powers. We cannot shoulder other people's afflictions and pains – which is exactly what Jesus did. He carried our physical infirmities when he suffered for sin on the Cross. Like every blessing, healing comes through the Cross. Christ died for others. We cannot do that; only Jesus, the Son of God, could. Only he has the right to save and heal others. To think that when a healing takes place God is signalling his approval of our holiness is an offence to the One who redeemed us.

The teaching that holiness brings power dates back to medieval times. To seek God men and women became hermits, anchorites, fasting and neglecting their natural physical needs and appetites. They walked through the streets conspicuous for their neglected appearance and were regarded as saints. People touched their clothes in the hope of being healed and drew threads from their ragged garments to carry as a charm against their sicknesses. The truth is that these men and women shut themselves off from everybody and concentrated on saving their own souls. The needs of the world outside were largely forgotten. It was the old error of salvation by works, sanctification by works and power by works, and God never blesses that.

If signs and wonders come from God alone, then we cannot be showmen. Christian services are not exhibitions of our religious stature. Christ gives us the victory that he won on the Cross. *"From the fullness of his grace have we all received"* – that is, "out of" his fullness we receive our supply. *"We have this treasure* [this power] *in jars of clay to show that this all-surpassing power is from God and not from us"* (2 Corinthians 4 :7). That power flows out as it flows in, the overflowing of God through mortal lives. Once we start exalting ourselves as miracle men, God will let us try it! We soon find how empty we are. We may as well try to wash one hand without the other getting wet as try to minister to the afflicted without the Lord.

> We cannot generate power by our own holiness and virtue.

Actually, I am thankful for that. If anyone looked to me and not to Jesus for healing, I would feel like the King of Israel in 2 Kings 5. He received a letter from the king of Aram about his army chief Naaman who had leprosy. In that letter he asked the King of Israel to cure Naaman. The king of Israel panicked. *"Am I God?"* he asked. *"Can I kill and bring back to life? Why does this fellow send someone to me to be cured of leprosy? See how he is trying to pick a quarrel with me!"* (2 Kings 5:7).

By faith and love we focus the sun of righteousness risen with healing in his wings. That is, we focus on a person's need, caring and believing for that that one individual.

But Elisha the prophet heard of the coming of Naaman, and through his prophetic ministry Naaman was healed. What was the result? Naaman said, *"Now I know that there is no God in all the world except in Israel"* (2 Kings 5:15).

Apparently no one except Christ has seen everybody healed. I have come to understand that if some people in the crowd are not healed, it is not my responsibility, however much it grieves me, or however much I am criticised. It is God's business. I leave it with him. The same applies not only to healing but also to all our work. As the hymn says, "I leave with the Lord my endeavour". God promised to bless his word, save souls, restore the stricken, and he does – but apparently not everybody. That is his business. I claim no healing ability for myself. God himself knows the whys and wherefores of the things, which we as humans cannot understand.

Signs and Wonders and human Motivation

Despite what I have said about the power – and the glory – belonging to God, it is also true that God does nothing without us. But who? When? There are issues we dare not overlook.

First there is the question of motive. Why do we want to heal the sick? The concept of power is attractive. Some covet the power to walk down the street distributing cures right and left or emptying hospital wards. Many people receive a wonderful sense of greatness if they possess power. Some crave political or financial power and others miracle power. Is there a difference? Will God encourage that kind of dubious motivation?

> To heal the sick calls for us to hate sickness.

What motivated Jesus? Love – nothing more or less. The first three gospels all describe his compassion. In John the word "compassion" is not used; it becomes "love". To heal the sick calls for us to hate sickness. Are we sick of people being sick? When people tell us they have some bad ailment, it is easy to say, "I'll pray for you". But here is how the writer of Psalm 35 reacted when he heard of even an unfaithful friend being ill: *"When they were ill, I put on sackcloth, and humbled myself with fasting. When my prayers returned to me unanswered, I went about mourning as though for my friend or brother. I bowed my head with grief as though weeping for my mother."* That man was in harmony with the spirit of Jesus. Without love we are nothing – as we are told in 1 Corinthians 13.

> Faith and love are like a magnifying glass.
> We hold a glass up to the sun and focus its rays on one tiny spot and there is intense heat.
> By faith and love we focus the sun of righteousness risen with healing in his wings.

"Faith works by love" is the message of Galatians 5:6. Faith and love are like a magnifying glass. We hold a glass up to the sun and focus its rays on one tiny spot and there is intense heat. By faith and love we focus the sun of righteousness risen with healing in his wings (or beams). That is, we focus on a person's need, caring and believing for that that one individual. Love is always individual, no matter how many sit around the table. James 5:16 instructs us, *"Pray for each other so that you may be healed."*

The love of God is always individual. *"I have loved Jacob,"* God said (Malachi 1:2). Jesus did not love the people, but he did love John, Lazarus and *"his own"* (John 13:1). Matthew 10 tells the tale of a rich young man who came to Jesus; *"Jesus looked at him and loved him"* (verse 21) and invited him to be a follower. Paul did not say that God loved us, but that he *"loved me and gave himself for me"* (Galatians 2:20), a clear expression of God's focus on the individual. Christ said, *"As the Father has loved me, so have I loved you"* (John 15:9). In his great prayer in John 17:26, he tells God of his purpose, his motivation, in making him known: *"that the love you have for me may be in them"*. Christ was the one and only "well-beloved" Son. His instruction is *"Love each other as I have loved you"* (John 15:12).

Although masses of people came to Jesus for healing, the gospels give as many stories about individuals as possible. When a woman stole up behind him and reached out her hand to touch the hem of his clothing, she was healed, as it were, anonymously. But Jesus never heals anonymously. It is a gift, which comes with his personal signature, so on this occasion he stopped in his tracks. He was on his way to a sick girl who was dying, her father agitating for him to get there urgently, but he would not move on until the woman had identified herself. Perhaps she thought he was going to reprimand her, but he merely wanted to given personal confirmation of her healing. Think of the way the Bible gives space to a wretched runaway slave like Onesimus; that great Apostle Paul wrote an immortal letter to get him forgiveness and restoration! Amazing love! Where do you find stories like that in other holy books?

The word for love in the New Testament is "agape", and originally it is thought to have been a word for a selective love, an attachment between two individuals only. Certainly that is what it means in Scripture. God loved the world, but his love is not a generalised love for people en masse but great love for each one. As Jesus put it, God knows the finest detail about us; the very hairs of our head are numbered. The Bible is built on the lives of individuals on whom God beamed his spotlight.

But how is God going to heal people today? Mainly as individuals. In our campaign crowds, it would be impossible

> The Bible is built on the lives of individuals on whom God beamed his spotlight.

to lay hands on every needy soul, but we do invite them to the platform when they have been healed to confirm our one-to-one joy and interest. Healing should happen between friends, for that way God's individual love is shown. We love because he loves; *"God has poured out his love into our hearts by the Holy Spirit"* (Romans 5:5). That is the personal contact sick people have with the Lord who loves them, through others. He needs many of us because there are many individuals he wants to heal. No matter how many sit at the table of the Lord, we are all special, and the Psalmist strikes the right note when he says *"The Lord is my shepherd. You prepare a table before me in the presence of my enemies"* (Psalm 23).

Signs and Wonders are Powertools for a serious Purpose

Perhaps many who listen to me preaching or who are reading this feel like Elisha the prophet who at first saw no wonders. But he came eventually to be one of the few people in ancient Israel whom God used in a spectacular way. Anyone who aspires to be a man or woman of power should consider carefully the steps taken by Elisha. He first served humbly as a menial servant. No one ever anointed him. Yet Elisha considered no price too great to be allowed to serve as he saw Elijah doing. He sacrificed everything, and persistently followed Elijah from one place to the next. Each place was relevant and significant as he tracked Elijah with determination. Finally he took over where Elijah left off, although his ministry had its own characteristics.

I have said that good works are not the way to power. But God is unlikely to grant any of us a gifted ministry unless we are prepared for the hard work involved and for the kind of dedication that demands

God loved the world, but his love is not a generalised love for people en masse but great love for each individual.

twenty-four hours a day, every day for the whole of our life. The gifted will never have rest from the work into which their gifts thrust them. Are you prepared? I will leave you with that question.

Christ will reign as Lord over all kings and all lords. This is the promise of God, and his schemes are faultless. Studying the divine strategy for world salvation is absolutely fascinating. In this chapter I want to convey something of God's plan to put his Son on the Throne.

I have headed this article Operation Pentecost. Pentecost is the code word for victory and implies the active involvement of the Holy Spirit. The Spirit is God's great secret for ultimate world deliverance. We must first understand clearly that God has a blueprint for the world; then we need to know who the Holy Spirit is and how he is going to bring about the will of God on earth.

The Secret of the nameless Name

First, who is the Holy Spirit, the Spirit of Pentecost? When God came to Manoah the father of Samson, he said, *"Why do you ask my name?"* (Judges 13:18). Does the Spirit of God have a real name? We don't know. Actually, Manoah did not find out, either! The question was clue enough to the identity of the speaker. Now, if we look back to the languages in which the Bible was first written, we find that "spirit" simply means "wind" or "breath". In New Testament Greek the word for spirit was pneuma. This word had been used by the Greeks centuries earlier to mean the nature of life, which was a ready-made term for the Holy Spirit.

More important than knowing a hidden name, it is vital to understand the character of the Holy Spirit. First, I must stress that he is not a ghost. Older Bibles used to speak of the Holy Ghost. It gave a lot of people the wrong idea. They imagined a phantom hovering around in churches or graveyards, or perhaps a mysterious ambience in places of worship producing a "sense" of sacredness. (A "numinous" quality some people call it.) In ancient cathedrals and great churches the splendour of the soaring architecture can generate a feeling of awe; it is not necessarily God's Spirit. Nonetheless, many of us would testify that the Spirit does indeed have a personal aura. Where he is at work, especially, we may feel his closeness. That brings home the point: rather than wafting around as a mystical presence, the Holy Spirit is made manifest in his activity.

It is critical to accept that that word "Spirit" itself implies action. The people of ancient Israel linked God with things they saw happening and drew a parallel between his invisible power and the invisible force of the wind. In fact, it sometimes was the wind causing miraculous events, God's wind or breath as when the Red Sea parted to let the Israelites through. Bible commentaries sometimes state that ruah ("spirit" in Hebrew) means "air in motion". I think that "air" is an unlikely choice of word. In fact, I wonder if the people of old even knew there was such a thing as air. At least, they never talked that way. To them where there was movement, there was God: *"God rides on the wings of the wind"* (Psalm 104:3). Even when they drew breath, they talked of God breathing the breath of life into them each living moment (see Psalm 104:29-30).

Israel credited everything that happened to God. Although several prophetical books make no mention of the Spirit, the prophets saying they spoke "by the word of the Lord"; the New Testament says that they *"spoke as they were moved by the Holy Spirit"* (2 Peter 1:21).

In the New Testament the only person to be identified with air is Satan, *"the prince of the power of the air"* (Ephesians 2:2). Air has pressure, atmosphere. That is the best Satan can do, conjure up an atmosphere and build up pressure. God does not do that.

To know God is to take on board what Jesus told us: *"God is Spirit* [pneuma]. *The wind blows wherever it pleases. So it is with everyone born of the Spirit"* (John 4:24, 3:8). The Spirit is therefore an ever-present life force.

Spiritual Photosynthesis

The Scriptures are an essential factor in world redemption so they were not left entirely to human agency. When writing to Timothy, Paul used the word "theopneustos", meaning "divinely breathed in": *"All Scripture is God-breathed"* (2 Timothy 3:16). God breathed into the Word,

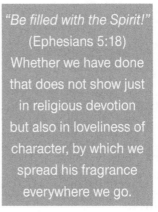

"Be filled with the Spirit!" (Ephesians 5:18) Whether we have done that does not show just in religious devotion but also in loveliness of character, by which we spread his fragrance everywhere we go.

which absorbed his divinity like a flower drinking in wind and sunshine. Then the flower breathes the sunshine out again in the form of beauty and fragrance. We call the botanical process photosynthesis. Something like spiritual photosynthesis should take place in every Christian life. *"Be filled with the Spirit,"* we are told (Ephesians 5:18). Whether we have done that does not show just in religious devotion but also in loveliness of character, by which we spread his fragrance everywhere we go (2 Corinthians 2:14). The chief work of the Holy Spirit is us! He makes us his agents. God grant that we look as if we are! It is how the world will know about him.

I have said that the Holy Spirit is not just a pervading atmosphere in a church. It is common enough to try to create a good atmosphere in our meetings, though it is a mistake to think that that is the same as the Holy Spirit. An "atmosphere" arises from our mutual attitudes. When the 120 disciples came together on the Day of Pentecost, there was surely a lovely spirit, congenial and cordial, among them. There would be nothing like it anywhere else in Jerusalem, and certainly not in the Temple. Christian fellowship is incomparable. The disciples might have been well satisfied with the unique and pleasant experience, and would have probably wanted to make it a regular thing, say every Sunday morning, and in fact they do seem to have enjoyed such pleasant fellowship for some time.

> Christian fellowship is a precious and needed experience. In Christ we have an extraordinary privilege of fellowship.

A new Dynamism

Then came *"a mighty rushing wind"* (Acts 2:2). A gale does not usher in a "sacred" atmosphere; it generally changes things radically. The disciples were jolted out of their routine. A new dynamism put them on their feet to face the people in Jerusalem, and a startled and staring multitude heard the first gospel message ever preached.

Christian fellowship is a precious and needed experience. It is good for brothers to live together in unity (Psalm 133:1). In Christ we have an extraordinary privilege of fellowship. But that sense of oneness has an objective and is not an end in itself. *"The Father is always at his work to this very day, and I, too, am working,"* Jesus said (John 5:17). The Spirit works

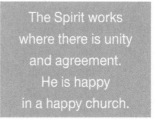

The Spirit works where there is unity and agreement. He is happy in a happy church.

where there is unity and agreement. He is happy in a happy church. We are brought together in the bonds of the love of Christ for his works, and shaped to be an instrument of righteousness in the hand of God.

We must recognise who our co-worker is. The Holy Spirit did not invade the world from a mystic's cell but on Pentecost. He came on the first day of the week – the working week, the world of business and clamour – and not on the quiet Sabbath. The real world of work and trade is where the Holy Spirit moves. That is how we picture the Holy Spirit, the God of Pentecost. Now that we know where to find him, we can turn to see his work.

The dark Land

Before Christ the world was enemy-held territory. The
lights had all gone out, every nation was steeped in idolatry.
Spiritual darkness thick with ignorance and cruel superstitions prevailed throughout the world. The night had one
star and that glittered only restlessly in the blackness. It
shone in little Israel. Three quarters of that nation, too, had
succumbed to the overwhelming darkness and had chosen
the way of the world, thoughtlessly casting off their dis-
tinctive mark of life in the knowledge of God.

The brightness of human intelligence was unable to dispel
the darkness. Rome built a glittering empire with its great
capitals, roads and architecture. The Greeks produced the
most brilliant and searching intellects and the most splen-
did art, yet their lives were crude, pathetic and devoid of all
certainty. They invented gods who became Frankenstein
monsters, tyrants, bent on making their daily lives as dif-
ficult as could be. Nowhere, on land or on sea, did anyone
have the slightest notion of the living God and his warm
heart of love.

The Genesis Story

How did the whole globe come to ride in such a pitch
black night? Behind it is the Genesis story. God gave
Adam dominion over the earth. He walked alone as king
of the world. But then came the great disaster – at the
hands of the Serpent, the tempter. Adam gave in to temp-
tation and, in so doing, surrendered his authority to the

usurper. The world became occupied territory, dominated by the powers of darkness, with Satan *"the prince of this world"*, as Jesus described him (John 12:31). God no longer walked in the garden he had

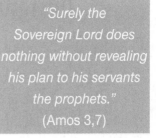

"Surely the Sovereign Lord does nothing without revealing his plan to his servants the prophets."
(Amos 3,7)

made. Heaven was pushed far away and communication ceased. Few people prayed. In Noah's day there were only eight of them. People built a tower to reach heaven but they did it to show off, not to find God. The endeavour ended in confusion, nobody knowing what anybody else said. The world was cut off from its Creator and estranged from its very self.

The spirit of the prophets should equip us all. We are to be the marching troops of the coming victory of the Kingdom of God.

However, there have always been secret agents, men and women of great daring, who have been smuggled in on behalf of resistance and governments aiming for freedom. They have known the minds of their governments and their secret work has contributed to the future victory. Something like that went on in the ancient pagan world, too. God had his agents: the prophets of Israel. *"Surely the Sovereign Lord does nothing without revealing his plan to his servants the prophets"* (Amos 3:7). They were his secret agents behind enemy lines and spoke only what he told them speak. Their power and authority came from God: Micah said, *"I am full of power by the Spirit of the Lord"* (Micah 3:8). That is how things were until Christ came to earth.

Operation Kingdom

When Jesus made his first public appearances, he made some astounding declarations: *"The Kingdom of God is near."* He later added a few more details, saying, *"If I drive out demons by the finger of God, then the kingdom of God has come to you"* (Luke 11:20). Now that was something to think about! God was no longer somewhere beyond the darkness. Christ personally spearheaded the kingdom and demonstrated its intention by casting out demons that is by directly attacking the evil entities behind world oppression and idolatry. Israel had prayed, *"Lord, rend the heavens and come down"* (Isaiah 64:1) and, beyond all they ever imagined, that that is precisely what God did.

The Kingdom of God has invaded the darkness of earth. It was not an excursion or a mere reconnaissance trip, but God's D-Day. With Christ at the forefront, deliverance, light and truth broke though on to the earth. Jesus said, *"I saw Satan fall like lightning from heaven"* (Luke 10:18). The invincible Holy Spirit was at work, no longer through secret agents, but now operating boldly in the streets and synagogues. Whatever Jesus did, he did by the Holy Spirit (see Acts 10:38, Luke 4:18).

We have four gospels and evangelical preachers make great use of John because it has great salvation verses. But in Matthew, Mark and Luke, Jesus demonstrates the Kingdom and hints at something not then fully revealed, that every one of us should ask for the Holy Spirit. The spirit of the prophets should equip us all. We are to be the marching troops of the coming victory of the Kingdom of God. The Spirit is our munitions of war against hell.

John's gospel is certainly the book of salvation but it is also supremely the book of the Holy Spirit. In chapters 14, 15 and 16 Jesus impresses upon the disciples that he must go to the Father so that he can send the Spirit. It is "expedient", Jesus said – for the good of each one of us. If the Spirit had not come, the world would be back where it was in the days of ancient Israel, in a state of darkness with no demons cast out, no crippled, blind or sick people healed, and no thousands converted.

However, Christ had begun the invasion by the Spirit, and now it must go on. The book of Acts tells the story of the first advances of the Kingdom as the disciples realised the power of the Spirit bestowed upon them. As I have already said, we are encouraged to be filled with the Spirit. Those early disciples began the work. We continue it.

We are not secret agents. Jesus explained that the prophets prophesied until John the Baptist (Matthew 11:13). Our work is different; we are not to pronounce judgment but to announce the good news: not gloom and doom for the nations, but the hope of the gospel – abundant life. We are part of the kingdom forces, clothed with the same spirit of the prophets but for a different work, that of proclaiming the Kingdom. We know what the world is, what darkness is, what evil,

> Repent and be converted! This is not a suggestion, but an ultimatum of love.

treachery, betrayal, wickedness and cruelty are. We are not here simply to tell people we are against all of that – who isn't? – but to offer them the key to let them out of the whole ghastly prison and to lead victims out of its dark depths and fetid atmosphere into the glorious freedom of the Kingdom of God.

We are not building strongholds – we are pulling them down! This is neither trench warfare, nor is it a blitzkrieg. Ours is a work which involves relentlessly easing forward, advancing in righteousness and godliness. The Spirit *"will convict the world of guilt with regard to sin and righteousness and judgement"* (John 16:8). The Kingdom forces are here until Jesus himself appears among us as our Captain to bring about final Holy Spirit victory. We are not here to match intellect with intellect, or argument with argument, but, by the Spirit, as ambassadors to offer the world terms of surrender, repent and be converted. It is not a suggestion, but an ultimatum of love. It will not come about by brute force. *"Not by might nor by power, but by my Spirit,"* says the Lord Almighty (Zechariah 4:6).

The Bible and the Holy Spirit

Jesus said, *"Suppose a king is about to go to war. Will he first not sit down and consider whether he is able to oppose the one coming against him?"* (Luke 14:31)

Believers should know whether they are able to oppose the devil. Do they have what it takes to "fight the good fight of faith" and outmatch the forces of godlessness? Many

Christians simply don't know. They hope and pray but as no surging conviction of divine power grips them, they have an uncomfortable feeling that something about their lives is the problem. With this I want to give you some encouraging assurance. We are not without our spiritual munitions.

Just look carefully at what Paul said that he prayed in Ephesians 1:18-19, that *"the eyes of your heart may be enlightened in order that you may know … his incomparably great power for us who believe"*. That is the situation regarding power in the New Testament; the crux of the matter is not whether we possess a personal supply of it or not, but whether we know in our hearts the power of God "for us". We do not draw on what we have but on what God has. Let me show you what I mean.

> We do not draw on what we have but on what God has.

3 wonderful Facts

1. No one who has been born again is without the Holy Spirit. A Christian believer is born of the Spirit and exists by the daily and ceaseless operation of that same Spirit. God never abandons his children like orphans, without the Holy Spirit. He wants us to live like his children, and he makes sure of that by the Spirit. The Holy Spirit himself is the mark of a Christian: *"If anyone does not have the Spirit of Christ, he does not belong to Christ"* (Romans 8:9).

2. The Holy Spirit is not an extra for extra good Christians. Jesus said that it was for our own good that he would withdraw and make space for the Holy Spirit (John 16:7). The coming of the Spirit, indispensable for our common need, fulfilled the tremendous act of the ascension. To some people's way of thinking, Holy Spirit power is a luxury, rather like caviar and pheasant – reserved for the highly privileged. Jesus did not speak like that; he compared the Spirit to such ordinary things as bread, fish and eggs (Luke 11:11-13), telling us that the Spirit is for ordinary people, including children. Peter later proclaimed the same common blessing for all people: *"The promise is for you and your children and for all who are far off – for all whom the Lord our God will call"* (Acts 2:39).

3. With the Holy Spirit, God ensured that his work would be done. Salvation and everything else became possible with the Spirit. He is the primary factor behind all Christian service. God's work could no more be done without the Holy Spirit than an artist could create a masterpiece without paint or a sculptor could carve a statue without stone. God has no "Plan B" without the Spirit to accommodate people who want to work on their own.

> The Holy Spirit helps us but only as we help him. The work is his.

This is where we must get our viewpoint right. We should not look on the Spirit as an extra, something that it is better to have than not, for every undertaking is pointless without him. The Holy Spirit helps us but only as we help him. The work is his. Some see the Spirit only as the Comforter. He is indeed the

Comforter, but not solely to make us comfortable on life's journey. Indeed, there would be no journey without him – without his power we could not even leave the airport. I know some do not consider themselves important enough for the Holy Spirit. That is not for anyone to say. We all need the Spirit, and the Holy Spirit makes us important.

Understanding the Holy Spirit

I want to go on now to open up more truth about the Spirit from the Word. Understanding is not a matter of filling our heads with knowledge, but of allowing truth to stimulate our faith and stir our hearts.

Take the Temple of Solomon. No human being lived there; it was God's dwelling place. God's dwelling place today is with his people. They are the new Temple, and he makes his home with them (John 14:17).

> The Holy Spirit has no place in this world except with his people, believers, and without their welcome he would be homeless.

The Spirit is not given to the world, but to all who are in Christ. When Jesus was baptised in Jordan, the Holy Spirit came down on him as a dove. Noah had a dove in the ark. He sent it out, but it came back because it found no resting place other than the ark. The Holy Spirit has no place in this world except with his people, believers, and without their welcome he would be homeless. But is he welcome everywhere, just as he is, full of fire and energy, coming in like a mighty gust of wind? Or is he only welcome as they perceive him, silent, cool, unobtrusive and soothing?

Christianity is the gift of the Holy Spirit. When Jesus began his earthly ministry, he was full of the Holy Spirit and mighty works followed. Nothing like it had ever been known before. Many acknowledge the validity of Christian faith as a doctrine or as a religious system and even express approval of its morals and ethics, but Christianity is more than all of this. Fundamentally it is the supernatural breaking into our mundane lives by the Spirit of God. Jesus did not have a lot to say about evangelical doctrine; he stressed the importance of entering the Kingdom by faith and receiving the Holy Spirit.

Ancient Israel had no promise of the Holy Spirit. Jesus said, *"Ask and you will receive"* (John 16:24). This was a new idea; the only thing like it in Old Testament times was in one striking pre-emption picture when Elisha asked Elijah for *"a double portion of your spirit"* (2 Kings 2:9). It was a geo-celestial change, affecting earth and heaven and announced by John the Baptist, the greatest and last prophet of the age of the Law of Moses. He said, *"I baptise with water, but he* [Christ] *will baptise with the Holy Spirit and with fire"* (Luke 3:16).

The written law had no intrinsic power to bring people into line with its commands, even though it was carved by God on tablets of stone. But the law of Christ is the Spirit, a life force operating on desire and will and purpose (see Romans 8:2). Moses' law comprised only legal obligations.

> Jesus stressed the importance of entering the Kingdom by faith and receiving the Holy Spirit.

Christ's law is about channelling instinctive desire. It is the difference between a forced marriage and a love match.

The Spirit in the Book of Acts

Is the book of Acts just history or is it more of an instruction manual? The book of Acts tells us how the Christian era began and what it was like. The disciples are seen discovering the tremendous potential of the outpoured Spirit of Pentecost. More than once God took the initiative to show them what the Holy Spirit could do, and they found themselves doing by the Spirit things that had never been done before. Jesus had said, *"Anyone who has faith in me will do what I have been doing. He will do even greater things than these, because I am going to the Father"* (John 14:12). Nobody had done what Jesus

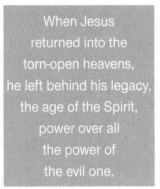

When Jesus returned into the torn-open heavens, he left behind his legacy, the age of the Spirit, power over all the power of the evil one.

did but when the Day of Pentecost turned those Galilean fishermen into channels of the Holy Spirit, they did what no prophet had ever done – they brought multitudes to repentance, opened blind eyes and deaf ears, and cast out evil spirits.

Jesus had come into the world; the ancient cry for God to rend the heavens and come down had been answered. When Jesus returned into the torn-open heavens, he left behind his legacy, the age of the Spirit, power over all the power of the evil one.

The days of the apostles were a great time of power. It is a challenge to all who go out with the Word. Was it the peak of Holy Spirit activity? Of course, apostles sent out personally by Jesus were the key workers. Is Acts an account of an explosion and demonstration of the pristine power of the Holy Spirit, never to be repeated? I wonder. That might well be our conviction, but we would be unable to find a single word in Acts – or indeed in the whole New Testament – to support such a theory. What may seem reasonable to us needs Scripture to make it valid. Were the events recorded in Acts an extra special display of power which took place at that time and which God later toned down?

When interpreting Scripture, such as the book of Acts, we must take care to remember God's character. He is faithful, true, unwavering, unchanging, never making special exertions. He has no peaks and troughs of power, he *"does not change like shifting shadows"* (James 1:17). He puts on no special shows. See God at any time and that is what he always is. Would a changeless God rise up for 30 years to extraordinary performances while the apostles were around, and then when they had gone, change his tactics to more moderate works? Did he do special favours just for them?

The book of Acts, like all Scripture is a revelation of an unchanging God. It is written to encourage us to trust him. Does it make sense for the book of Acts to be about exceptional happenings? Is God a God of exceptions? No, on the contrary. Acts is the Word of God to us, the first record showing us what happens when we have faith in Christ. It is normative – a pattern for what should always be.

If our Christian experience is different from what we read in Acts, do we have a new religion? Are we different from the people in Acts? The purpose of Acts is the same as all Scripture, to reveal God, what he is, changeless, pursuing the same objectives with undiminished purpose: the salvation and healing of the world. The apostles had no superior power. They had the same

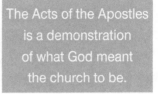

The Acts of the Apostles is a demonstration of what God meant the church to be.

Holy Spirit as all who ask. There is no greater power.

The Acts of the Apostles is a demonstration of what God meant the church to be. Our circumstances present different opportunities and call for different responses, as in Acts, but the same God went out with the disciples confirming his word by the signs that accompanied it. He has never retired.

What is Truth?

You will know the truth.

John 8:32

To do a job properly you need the proper tools. We search the skies with a telescope not a microscope and fish with a net not a necktie. The mind, our intellect, leads us to scientific discoveries but it cannot discover God or the truth. It is the wrong instrument for that. Brainpower does not operate in that area.

That is not a new idea; Paul the apostle said, *"The world through its wisdom did not know God"* (1 Corinthians 1:21). He was talking about men who have left their mark in history, the Greek philosophers, Thales, Anaximander and Anaximenes, who lived 600 years before Christ, and the members of the Socratic school of thought so greatly admired in modern academic circles. These and many more failed to find anything we could call truth or God by applying their intellect.

Jesus said, *"I am the truth"* (John 14:6). In other words, truth is not a proposition but a person. The philosophers have never got as far as that in their thinking – how could they? Some Greeks came to Jesus and he turned their views upside down by referring to his own death and resurrection (John 12:23-25). That is where thinking really begins – at the Cross. Otherwise we are off on the wrong foot. Paul saw that God had *"made foolish the wisdom of the world"*

(1 Corinthians 1:20) by the divine wisdom of the Cross of Christ. That is the yardstick by which all human thought is judged.

Many say they are seeking but are they really? They are living in darkness and do not know what to look for. If the truth bounced up and hit them smack in the face, they would not recognise it! They usually keep clear of places where they might actually find God. Scholars have made a great mystery of "epistemology", the theory of how we know. We know our own selves, we know others and we can know God. In fact, God has given us other faculties for discovery than just brains. We possess 5 senses, spiritual intuition, faith, feelings, moral judgment and intelligence and all can be ways to "know". By faith people everywhere make contact with resurrection life and come to know him who is the way, the truth and the life.

God is not imagination. Nor is he just our faith in him, although faith is the channel through which the Spirit of God can work. God is not accessible only to those with great minds. Some of life's greatest realities – music, poetry, beauty, desire, love and hope – have nothing to do with reason. God wants to be known and does not hide in thick books on theology that the average person cannot hope to understand. John the Apostle wrote to many who were illiterate, saying that they knew the truth: *"To* [those] *whom I love in the truth – and not I only, but also all who know the truth – because of the truth, which lives in us and will be with us for ever"* (2 John 1). To know the truth needs no university education.

Already found

Christians are not looking for the truth – they have already found it! What they are doing is exploring it. The truth is not an idea and is more than a revelation: it is an encounter. God, the Lord himself, comes to us. The truth turns out to be infinite. The Holy Spirit is the guide *"into all truth"* (John 16:13) and that truth is Christ Jesus. *"The Spirit of truth … will bring glory to me by taking from what is mine and making it known to you"* (John 16:13-14). The truth will nurture us and satisfy us or else it is not the truth. Speculations cannot feed my everlasting soul. The truth is the bread and the water of life and our everlasting goal.

> God wants to be known and does not hide in thick books on theology that the average person cannot hope to understand.

It is so strange. The world's quest for the chalice of truth has led to nothing, so they make the best of it by keeping the quest going, just seeking and never finding! They would appear to believe what Robert Louis Stevenson said, "To travel hopefully is a better thing than to arrive, and the true success is to labour". A modest aim, perhaps, but futile! The name of that game is philosophy, always exploring but never arriving at any final conclusion. There is no sign of the truth and no absolutes, any ideas are just there until something "better" comes along. It is a merry-go-round kept moving by new thinkers disagreeing with previous thinkers.

By contrast, the Bible is sure-footed as it leads us along the paths of truth and righteousness. Its 66 books, 1,189 chapters and 733,693 words are written not in search of truth but to bring its light to bear on our lives, exposing the dirty corners. Scripture is surrounded by seas of uncertainty but sails along majestically, never off course, driven by the winds of divine inspiration. The same waters are thrashed by the wise of this world in futile endeavour. They *"are coming to nothing"* as Paul put it.

> *"What is truth?"* Pontius Pilate asked Jesus. He sighed and turned away. He thought nobody knew. But he was standing face to face with the truth and could not see it!

"What is truth?" Pontius Pilate asked Jesus (John 18:38). He sighed and turned away. He thought nobody knew. Charles Spurgeon said that the mark of the scholar was an ability to miss the obvious. Jesus told Pilate, *"For this I came into the world, to testify to the truth"* (John 18:37). Pilate was standing face to face with the truth and could not see it! Jesus is the rock-solid basis of all truth and reality. When we discover him, we discover everything, for ever. Whether simpleton or genius, everyone can know someone and they can know Jesus. In that case, a cat may indeed look at a king, as the saying goes.

Jesus said, *"I am the truth."* The idea that truth was a person, that truth could be incarnate, was far from human thought. How could anybody think it? Paul debated with the Stoics and Epicureans (Acts 17:16-34) and before them there had been the seven wise men of Greece, Sophists, Cynics, Plato, Aristotle and so on. One of them, Pythagoras, declared that it was impossible to know truth by theology.

He invented a religion of his own in which greatest sin was eating beans! Aristotle wrote about human conduct in his ethics but without a spark of concern for people in the ups and downs of real, everyday life. He thought that God did not know we existed and that he could not love us.

The apostle Paul said, *"We speak a message of wisdom, but not the wisdom of this age or of the rulers of this age, who are coming to nothing"* (1 Corinthians 2:6). They certainly are "coming to nothing" for their best thoughts propounded only the three ideological values of truth, beauty and goodness. These values, including their concept of truth, were mere abstractions, bodiless notions. They meant nothing and did nothing for anybody. Against them Paul set the three great Christian values, *"faith, hope and love"* (1 Corinthians 13:13). These are the fundamental dynamics of existence, bringing us strength, meaning and challenge. Speaking to his disciples, Jesus said, *"You will know the truth"* (John 8:32) and indeed we do! It undergirds time and eternity and touches the springs of life.

> When we find Jesus, the great questions are not so much answered as become meaningless. He is the reason for everything. Jesus prayed to the Father, *"Your word is truth"* (John 17:17).

When we find Jesus, the truth, the great questions are not so much answered as become meaningless. He is the reason for everything. Jesus prayed to the Father, *"Your word is truth"* (John 17:17), and Jesus is the word. The Lord God of Israel was true and faithful. No heathen deity was remotely true, faithful or even moral.

Isaiah hammers away at that. Israel spoke of *"the true and living God"*, scorning the dumb idols of the nations.

> Jesus is the truth and everything he said is truth. When he said that anyone who believed in him would have life, it was not merely a bit of encouragement or even verbal assurance, but a statement about the order in which we live, God's order.

God is not only the true God, but the God of truth: *"Into your hands I commit my spirit; redeem me, o Lord, the God of truth"* (Psalm 31:5). What a wonderful thing to say – far beyond the wisdom of Egypt. It means that all truth comes from God. Therefore, what does not come from God is false. Anything we do or think that cannot be related to God, is a lie.

Without God in mind, nobody can be sure of anything. Uncertainty is almost a religious belief today. They call it "postmodernism". It is not politically correct to be sure of anything! We are expected to be uncertain about the gospel, out of politeness to other religionists! As if the truth were such an airy-fairy abstraction that we could pretend not to know the truth! We know what we know! The postmodern mood looks for no fixed truth, only flexible and relative opinion. This represents a tragic hollow at the heart of any nation, inhabited by bewildered souls.

The difficulty is that we do know. The gospel is the *"the word of truth"* (Ephesians 1:13, Colossians 1:5). Jesus is the truth and our Christian message is simply Christ. Paul seems to come across too strongly when he says that if anyone were to preach a different gospel from the one he preached, he would deserve to be eternally condemned (Galatians 1:8). Yet what else could possibly happen? If a man said two and two made ten, he would be in trouble. The truth is the truth and a man may as well try to knock a stone wall down with his head as deny it. Christ the Creator is at the seat of power at the heart of creation. Everything he did was an outward expression of the truth. His Cross and Resurrection are truth, locked into creation for ever. The stars in their courses are not surer.

Christ shouldered our sins when he hung on the Cross. That is the core word of truth, woven into the fabric of all eternity. Nothing could be truer, more real or more effective. This is the rock on which God built the world. If a bird can rest on a mountain and be secure, we can certainly rest on the truth of the crucified Jesus and be infinitely more secure.

Jesus is the truth and everything he said is truth. When he said repeatedly that anyone who believed in him would have life, it was not merely a bit of encouragement or even verbal assurance, but a statement about the order in which we live, God's order. His word is written in heaven and has become the very nature of things. He said, *"Whoever comes to me I will never drive away"* (John 6:37) and that is as much a fact of life as the law of gravity.

> Christ shouldered our sins when he hung on the Cross. That is the core word of truth, woven into the fabric of all eternity.

The compassion of Jesus is built into our world. It is a new law. He talked about many things, not church all the time, but human life, worry, patience, love, happiness, pride, greed, covetousness and faithfulness. All these things relate to him and to the truth. He knows how we frail mortals need help and he stands by to order our affairs according to truth and to show us how to live as he lived, the true way to live. There simply is no alternative way of truth. We delude ourselves if we look for it or try to live any other way. Why even try? Jesus said, *"I am the light of the world. Whoever follows me will never walk in darkness, but will have the light of life"* (John 8:12).

Worship God!

Revelation 22:9

Worship is the highest Activity of the human Spirit

Jesus sometimes opened his heart to women and told them things he had not revealed to his disciples. They found him once talking to a woman, and they marvelled, perhaps feeling left out of it? She was a non-Jew, a hated Samaritan and something of a social pariah, yet it was to her that He revealed revolutionary teaching on worship. We will look at that teaching as we move on.

> Worship is not a subject discussed in the New Testament, and we don't read that they had worship services.
> Be that as it may, it is inconceivable not to worship God. It is the background to all the Scriptures.

There are different words for worship but I looked at every one of the 200 worship references in the concordance and turned up in my Bible each of the 85 texts on worshipping God. In 39 Bible books the word does not occur, yet it occurs in 17 Old Testament and 10 New Testament books. Worship is not a subject discussed in the New Testament, and we don't read that they had worship services. Be that as it may, it is inconceivable not to worship God. It is the background to all the Scriptures.

Approaching the living God

The Old Testament book specially about approaching God is Leviticus, but it doesn't use the word 'worship' at all, and there's a reason. We know what personal worship is but in early Israel it was corporate, not an individual spiritual relationship towards God. The one exception is Jabez, named as different, *"more honourable than his brethren"* (1 Chronicles 4:9). Israeli people related to God together, as a race, as God's covenant people. Worship was national and performed by mass pilgrimages on the feast days or festival occasions where priests offered sacrifices for the nation. Things perhaps were influenced slowly after King David brought his religious genius to bear on the whole Divine scene. The marvel of his Psalm 51 is his sense of a relationship between God and himself.

> Unthankfulness is a judgment on our times. We can properly enjoy what we have only when we are thankful. Worshippers are never grousers.

When originally the tribes left Egypt and seemed to have little idea of thanks or worship – see Psalm 106 – they had served the gods of Egypt, but that meant no more than observing certain superstitions and bringing certain offerings. It was routine not a passion. They saw spectacular displays of Divine omnipotence under Moses, but were too awed to worship although they had bowed down before the Lord on first hearing from Moses. Exodus 12:27, There are many references to their false worship, such as before the golden calf. The Lord led them but they displayed only general dissatisfaction and rebellion. This failure became the Lord's major complaint against Israel. Paul quotes their murmuring for our admonition in 1 Corinthians 10:10.

Israel had to learn that God owed them nothing. They were in captivity to Babylon from about 600 BC and only when released some 70 years later from those miseries did they begin to appreciate God's goodness. Ezra gathered all the released captives together and read the book of the Law of Moses and they *"bowed their heads and worshiped with their faces to the ground"*. Their previous troubles had sprung almost directly from their unthankful attitude.

Worship a most important Function

The worship of God is a most important function in life, and an indispensable ingredient of happiness. There's no way to be glad if we are not thankful. Today, in affluent countries worship is not common. It is inexcusable. We are more blessed with earthly comforts than ever any Roman Emperor dreamed. Unthankfulness is a judgment on our times. Without worship our spirit is bankrupt. We can properly enjoy what we have only when we are thankful. Worshippers are never grousers.

Matthew records that eight times individuals dropped to the ground before Jesus in worship wherever they were. Perhaps people then had fewer inhibitions and were more child-like but these impulsive acts of worship were so genuine and beautiful one wishes it happened like that today. I notice that they expressed their worship without words, with their whole body, falling at Christ's feet.

On the occasion when Christ fed the 5,000, nobody showed any sign of worship or even common thanks. This miracle, Christ's greatest, was a mirror of God's care for the whole human race. Unfortunately, everyone seemed to miss its significance, even his disciples. Jesus had to ask if they even remembered it! This miracle provision was a flashback to the manna in the wilderness when the people began murmuring *"Our soul loathes this light bread"*. The God, who gave the manna and fed 5,000 and received no thanks, is the same God now who feeds the whole human race. How many offer him praise?

True Worship

Any relationship with God requires worship. Jesus taught us when we pray to begin *"Our Father who art in heaven, hallowed be thy name"*. Referring to King David again he knew the situation regarding worship in his nation. Early Israel had no churches, synagogues, house meetings, prayer meetings or places for the preaching of the Word. King David planned a central temple where worship would be offered day and night. What we call the Psalms of David seem to have been the hymn book of the Temple. He also probably set up the Temple rota of priests and choirs.

David's wonderful work set the form in which Israel could bring honour and praise to the Lord. It was excellent but it being necessarily routine it eventually deteriorated, and lost spiritual vitality. The prophets later warned that many going through the order of worship were hypocritical. Regular Christian services must take on some shape of form. We can participate, but the most exuberant occasion can be just a dead work. So much is enjoyable in church – popular music and songs, crowds, good fellowship, attractive buildings, and a good atmosphere. It is enriching. It is also God-honouring so long as it is a gesture of heart-love for Christ in spirit and truth. Otherwise it will mean only what God said through Isaiah *"This people draw near me with their mouth, and with their lips do honour me, but have removed their heart far from me"* Isaiah 29:13.

Coming now to what Jesus said to the woman at the well, *"Ye shall neither at this mountain nor at Jerusalem worship the Father ... but the true worshippers shall worship the father in spirit and in truth, for the Father seeks such to worship him"*. First, he did not say God is seeking worshippers. He said God seeks those who worship him in spirit and in truth. Now that word "spirit" should be the Spirit. We pray in the Spirit and worship and prayer go together,

God is not a shrine God, more in one place than another. The people who worship God in spirit and truth are those who walk in the way of the Lord.

Ephesians 6:18. Also *"The Spirit also helps our infirmities: for we do not know what we should pray for as we ought but the Spirit itself makes intercession for us"* Romans 8:26. We worship God through the Spirit. He prepares us to worship him in truth.

Jesus told the woman at the well that the time would come when people would not need to go to Samaria or Jerusalem to worship. God is not a shrine God, more in one

> Worship is love raised to its highest degree: love at white heat, love that persists through all weathers and circumstances. How would the world know we loved God if we never entered a place of worship to offer him our hearts devotion?

place than another. The people who worship God in spirit and truth are those who walk in the way of the Lord. It is a life stance, our lives committed to him and like the great spirits around the throne of God we are his worshippers day and night.

But there should be special moments to confess he is supreme in our lives and that we own no other Lord. Worship is love raised to its highest degree, love at white heat, love that persists through all weathers and circumstances.

A man who loves his wife will have special days, birthdays, anniversaries or even surprise days when he shows her in some special way his love for her. For anyone to say they love God and worship him, but never attend worship, is a sham. Abimelech discovered Rebekka was Isaac's wife because through a window he saw him fondling her. How would the world know we loved God if we never entered a place of worship to offer him our hearts devotion?

There are times to delight in the Lord or indulge. Psalm 37:4. "Delight" is used 15 times in the Psalms. It literally means have a good time worshipping God, praising him together with many more, exulting, singing, dancing. People in the world talk of "going to have a good time". They mean getting drunk. What a way of life! Paul says *"Be not drunk with wine wherein is excess but be filled with the Spirit. Speaking to yourselves in psalms and hymns and spiritual songs, singing and making melody in your heart to the Lord, giving thanks always for all things unto God and the Father in the name of the Lord, Jesus Christ."* God is the source of all joy, all pleasure, all music, all glory, and even of laughter. We should make worship an occasion, give Jesus our exclusive attention and *"look full in his wonderful face"*. Christians are in the world to be glad and rejoice, not to be agents of doom and gloom.

Many entering a place of worship switch off their smiles, as if everything therein is sombre, still, and mysterious. That is the picture of Christians millions have and therefore never attend a church. To delight in God we must be ourselves, natural, not putting on some holy pose. Jesus cleansing the temple illustrates that. He turned out the racketeers and the blind and lame came in and he healed them. Then children seeing the excitement ran in and began shouting Hosanna. In the courts of the house of the Lord it was considered children should make no noise, and now here they were breaking all rules in full throated praise, as Jesus quoted, *"out of the mouths of babes and sucklings thou has perfected praise"*. But the temple authorities didn't like it! *"Tell them to be quiet"* they told Jesus.

> God is the source of all joy, all pleasure, all music, all glory, and even of laughter. Christians are in the world to be glad and rejoice, not to be agents of doom and gloom.

Jesus that day made the Temple the place of jubilation it should be. John in his Revelation caught a glimpse of heaven and it was pretty much like that. Riotous happiness! That's the new song of the Lord, in every language, new keys, new melodies, and new harmonies, accompanied by the musical roar of the fount of life flowing for ever. It is no use planning for heaven if you want to be miserable.

Geared to God

God works, by prompting prayer. When God wants to do a certain thing, he inspires prayer that he may do it. He only works that way. In Genesis 20 we read the first healing story recorded in Scripture. The prayer of Abraham brought forgiveness and healing to the whole household of the Philistine chief, Abimelech. However, this was not Abraham's idea; it was the Lord's idea from the start. He told Abimelech to ask Abraham to pray for him to be healed. He inspired Abraham to pray and inspired Abimelech to expect Abraham's prayer to be answered. It was all of God. And by healing a heathen family, God had committed himself—he could never again be any different. The Lord had revealed what he was, and he could not go back on it. God shows himself by his deeds and his deeds do not stand in contrast to his nature.

God may not copy his own deeds. He rarely repeats himself, for he has an infinite store of new approaches and plans. He has shown himself to be the healer and that healing is what he wants to do. Never forget: What his deeds demonstrate is the unchanging

God may not copy his own deeds. He rarely repeats himself, for he has an infinite store of new approaches and plans.

heart and character behind them. He has the same love, the same will he always has had, and his deeds cannot violate his character.

The divine Imperative

What God is, is what he must do. God cannot be what he is and not do it. If he is love, he must love somebody. If he is a saviour he must save. He must heal, because he has revealed himself to be a healer.

In the gospel of John, this comes out in the imperatives of Jesus. When Jesus said, *"You must be born again"* (John 3:7), he meant that he himself must do it for us. We cannot rebirth ourselves. Only God can bring such a thing about. James 1:18 declares, *"He chose to give us birth through the word of truth."* Rebirth comes by the Word of truth, the gospel. If the world is to be saved, the people must hear the gospel. If they must hear the gospel, then somebody must preach it: *"How can they hear without someone preaching to them?"* (Romans 10:14).

People need the gospel, and their need creates a need in the heart of God: He needs to send us with the gospel. He knows we must be born again, and he can't just sit down on his throne and do nothing about it. That would be completely contrary to all he has ever done. God knows our need and is under compulsion to meet it.

Likewise, if we who are made in God's image know about the hungry in the world, we need to do something about it. Their need creates in us a need to help the needy. If you and I have plenty, then we cannot merely stand by and watch our neighbors die of starvation. The same is true of spiritual food. Our spiritual need lays a compulsion on the heart of God; our attitude toward others should be the same.

When Jesus said, *"You must be born again,"* it meant that he also had to say almost immediately, *"The Son of Man must be lifted up"* (John 3:14). He used the same word, "must." Our need becomes his need to meet our need. Jesus lived under a constant sense of the imperative will of God. He must save because we need to be saved. He said, *"I have other sheep,"* sheep that must be saved. *"I must bring them also"* (John 10:16).

This revelation of God becomes our basis for both faith and evangelism. The God of the Bible, our Lord Jesus Christ, the changeless one, will never let us down. We go at his bidding with our hand in his and we introduce him to a weary world.

Centred in God

Let me remind you that the initiative is not with us; it is with God. Behind everything is the moving Spirit of God. That being the case, we are either relevant or irrelevant to what God is doing.

God is our centre; not this world. People say that we Christians are eccentric. An eccentric object wobbles around a point that is off-centre. But that is what the Bible calls "the world." It is not believers, evangelists, witnesses or Christians who are eccentric, but the world. The world wobbles as it revolves around itself, but the believer is centred on God.

> The message from the Cross must not be related to this world, but the world must relate to the message of the Cross. Too bad for the world if it is not, for it will be judged at the Cross.

When people in the church talk about making the gospel relevant, they usually mean that we need to show that the gospel has something in common with the world of industry, entertainment and commerce. They have it backward. The question is not whether the message can be related to this world, but whether the world is willing to relate to the message of the Cross. Too bad for the world if it is not, for it will be judged at the Cross. If the world is not relevant to the gospel, then the world is drifting; it has no anchor.

Another thing I hear people say is that 'evangelists answer questions the world is not asking'. Thank God for that! We are giving answers, ready for when the world decides to ask the right questions. Because it is asking all the wrong questions, any answers would be equally wrong.

> To be geared to the world means turning our gospel into another form of materialism – just another way to rake in money and goods.

Relevance is a matter of position and focus. We are only relevant when we relate to what the Holy Spirit is doing. We are often told our ministry has to be geared to the times. This is nonsense. We are geared to God. The machinery of heaven is turning, wheels within wheels. It is the machinery of heaven, not of industry, that must be our concern. To be geared to the world means turning our gospel into another form of materialism – just another way to rake in money and goods. What makes us relevant is not whether our message fits the situation – *"Do not be conformed to this world,"* the Bible tells us (Romans 12:2) – but whether the situation corresponds to the truth of Christ. In fact, the world is of no importance if it does not relate to God.

Into the main Current

We need to get our priorities right. We either get into the mainstream of revelation – the love of God for a wasted world – or we drift into a backwater filled with debris of theological controversy and church politics. Our priority must be

> The Holy Spirit is given to make us witnesses, and his own work is to highlight the work of Christ and actuate it in human lives.

the same as that of the Spirit. Why is the Holy Spirit here? The Holy Spirit is given to make us witnesses, and his own work is to highlight the work of Christ and actuate it in human lives (see John 16:9-11; Acts 1:8). If we want to move in the Spirit, we need to get into that kind of activity because that is what he is doing.

Some people who talk about moving in the Spirit seem to think and act as if they are the ones moving the Spirit. This is not biblical: *"Who has directed the Spirit of the Lord, or as his counselor has taught him?"* (Isaiah 40:13). He is not moving secretly. He has not suddenly shot off in some new and unexpected direction only spotted by a few members of some spiritual elite. We still find God at work among people who are down: the sinful, the hopeless and the derelicts. Follow Jesus! That is a better expression than moving in the Spirit. Follow him and you will go where he goes, doing good and healing all who are oppressed by the devil (see Acts 10:38). Praise be to God.

366 DEVOTIONS
for every day of the year

"Mark my Word" is a carefully compiled collection of dynamic daily devotionals from the perceptive writings of Evangelist Reinhard Bonnke. Every day you will read sharp, personal, seasoned Biblical insights that have been comprehensively prepared (with thorough scriptural cross-referencing) to help you reap the full benefits from each of the life-changing applications found on every page. You will be enriched and encouraged. In this one volume you'll also discover a wealth of basic Bible background information and inspiration that you'll be able to absorb and apply at your own pace – on a daily basis.

With its simple, convenient, easy-to-read format, you can take this book anywhere and plunge in at any point – choosing to read specific indexed selections focused on a particular topic or category of interest – or read it through and use it as your personal daily devotional, daily Bible reading program, and Bible study guide. "Mark my word" will help you make the most of your Bible reading time as it strengthens your daily walk with the Lord.

418 pages • ISBN 3-935057-62-8

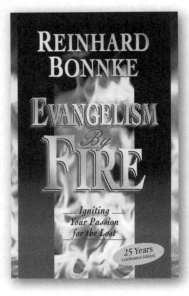

Evangelism by Fire
Igniting Your Passion for the Lost

Evangelism by Fire will give you an insight into the God-inspired anointing of Reinhard Bonnke. This book will fire your faith and give you the encouragement to believe God for the impossible. Evangelism by Fire is a powerful and practical presentation of the principles which the Lord has taught him over the years.

320 pages • ISBN 3-935057-19-9

Time is running out

There are more lost souls than ever – and less time than ever to save them. Now the evangelist's evangelist calls us – and helps us – to redouble our efforts to win over the world for Jesus. Reinhard Bonnke's unbridled passion for winning souls dates back to his youth.

He is acclaimed worldwide for a ministry that has one avowed, all-consuming purpose – plunder hell to populate heaven! Poignant, exhorting and uncompromising, this dramatic book combines the author's excitement for evangelism with his proven, effective techniques for reaching the lost of this world. It is a resounding call for each of us to reexamine our priorities, heed the call of Christ, preach the good news, and save people from hell.

252 pages • ISBN 3-935057-60-1

Mighty Manifestations
The Gifts and Power of the Holy Spirit

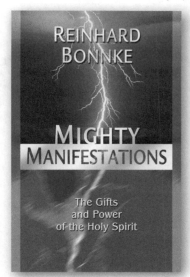

This book gives us a 'back to the Bible' examination of the spiritual gifts listed in 1 Corinthians 12. These are not given so that we may congratulate ourselves, or polish up our church's images, but to endorse the preaching of the Gospel to those around us. This is a book not only to increase our understanding, but to energise us for action.

298 pages
ISBN 3-935057-00-8

Faith – The Link with God's Power

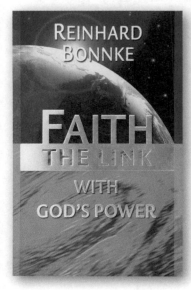

Some believe that simply having faith is an entitlement to blessing and prosperity. Others believe that faith in oneself is all that is needed in life. Still others contend that faith is a cosmic force that breeds superhuman, super-spiritual, invincible people. In this book, Reinhard Bonnke reveals the truth about faith towards God, drawing from his many years of personal study and experience.

292 pages
ISBN 3-935057-29-6